1678 - 1741

VIVALDI

1678-1741

VIVALDI

TIGER BOOKS INTERNATIONAL
LONDON

© 1995 Bookman International bv
    Houtweg 11, 1251 CR Laren (NH)
    The Netherlands

This book appears under the auspices of Euredition bv, Den Haag,
Netherlands

For this present English language edition: Todtri Productions Ltd.,
New York

Text: Jeroen Koolbergen
Translation: Van Splunteren/Burret
Lay-out: ADM, Pieter van Delft

This edition published in 1995 by Tiger Books International PLC,
Twickenham.

ISBN 1-85501-788-1

Introduction

The rediscovery of the composer Antonio Vivaldi began in September 1939 in the Italian city of Sienna. In the 19th century, musicologists who had studied the work of Johann Sebastian Bach already had pointed out Bach's admiration for Vivaldi. Bach reworked some 20 of the Italian composer's concertos and in so doing had evoked interest in him. This did not mean, however, that Vivaldi's music was of much interest to the general public.

September 1939 was a turning point. Various works by Vivaldi were performed over six days during a special musical week. They met with unprecedented success, a success which has continued right up to the present day, although the accent is heavily on Vivaldi's instrumental work, while his operas and oratorios are still largely neglected.

The concertos could not have been performed without previous archival research. After the first catalogue of all the printed works had been made in 1922, in 1927 the National Library of Turin pulled off a great coup with the purchase of 14 manuscripts of Vivaldi's music. These included 140 compositions of instrumental music, 12 operas, 29 cantatas, an oratorio, and other vocal compositions. These were probably Vivaldi's own collection which had wandered around through the centuries and had finally finished up in a monastery. Now, at last, they could finally be studied and published.

The 20th–century Italian composer, Dellapiccola, once said that Vivaldi had not written 450 concertos, but had written one concerto 450 times. This comment contains a grain of truth but is unfair to Vivaldi: his versatility, his desire for innovation, and his virtuosity will continue to appeal to music lovers.

Vivaldi's monogram

Apart from a few letters, hardly any documents which give an overall picture of Vivaldi's life and personality have survived. We do not even know exactly what he looked like. The portrait on the opposite page, by the Dutch lithographer François Morellon La Cave, is regarded as the "official" portrait, but is rather stereotyped. In 1723, two years earlier, Pier Luigi Ghezzi made a caricature sketch of the composer, who posed for him in Rome (see page 10). It is not certain that the third portrait (opposite the title page) actually is Vivaldi. But those who look very carefully will notice a lock of hair curling out from under the wig. It is red, and the composer had red hair...

It was once asserted that Antonio Vivaldi was descended from an old and illustrious family, traces of which could be found in the history of Genoa as far back as the early 12th century. The family had even produced a Doge of Genoa (a sort of duke and the highest official in the old republics of Genoa and Venice). Whether this was true or not, we know for certain that Vivaldi's grandfather, Agostino, was a baker in Brescia and he lived there until 1666. His son, Giovanni Battista (or Giambattista), born in 1656 or 1657, showed musical talent and was taken to Venice by his mother, Margarita, after the death of her husband. Information about Giovanni Battista, Vivaldi's father, is somewhat conflicting. On the day of his wedding to Camilla Calicchio he was described as a baker, while other sources suggest that he was a barber. Furthermore, in 1678, in the official baptismal certificate of his son Antonio, he was named "sonador," or instrumentalist.

In any event, Vivaldi's father was a musician – and a good one too – because on April 23, 1685, he was promoted to violinist in the San Marco orchestra where his honorarium was raised from 15 ducats to 25. At that time this prestigious ensemble was under the leadership of the well–known composer, Giovanni Legrenzi (1626–1690).

Still more is known about Giovanni Battista. He was called "Rossi" because of his red hair, a characteristic inherited by his son Antonio who would go through life bearing the nickname "the red priest." He was co–founder of the Santa Cecilia Society, which counted the best musicians in Venice, including Legrenzi, among its members. On September 30, 1729, when he was in his seventies, he asked for a year's leave from the San Marco orchestra so that he could accompany his son to Germany. Nothing more is known about Vivaldi's father after this point, except that he died in 1736.

It is only since 1962, when his baptismal certificate was discovered in the church of San Giovanni in Bragora, that we have known that Antonio Vivaldi was born in Venice on March 4, 1678. He was the eldest of the six children born to Giovanni Battista and Camilla Calicchio between 1678 and 1689. Little is known about the other five children, other than that two of Antonio's brothers had sons who were music copyists. One of them left Venice voluntarily, the other was banished after a quarrel with an aristocratic personage.

The official portrait of Antonio Vivaldi, by François Morellon La Cave, 1725 (Venice, private collection).

Immediately after his birth, Antonio became ill and for weeks his life was in danger. It was for this reason that he was not baptized until May 6 – at home by the midwife. On the day of his birth Venice was struck by an earthquake, and there is a theory that in her terror Vivaldi's mother vowed that her son would become a priest if things turned out for the best. It turned out, however, that Antonio was not particularly suited to fulfill this office...

Nothing is known about the young Vivaldi's teachers or about the kind of things he had to learn. On the other hand, all the information concerning his progress in training for the priesthood was noted. On September 18, 1693, when he was 15 years old, he was tonsured; between 1693 and 1696, he received the lower ordinations (ostiarius, lector, excorcist, and acolyte); on April 4, 1699, when he was twenty–one, he became a subdeacon; on September 18, 1700 he became a deacon; and on March 23, 1703, he was ordained a priest.

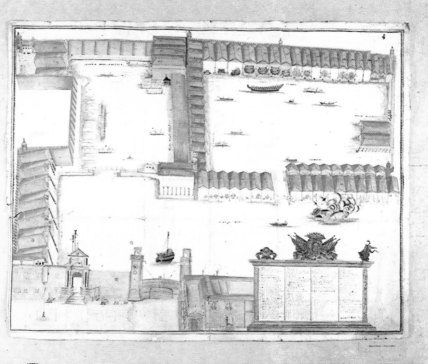

A caricature of Vivaldi, made in
Rome in 1723 by Pier Luigi
Ghezzi. Beneath the portrait are
the words: "The Red Priest, composer of music which the opera
performed in the Capranica
(theater) in 1723."

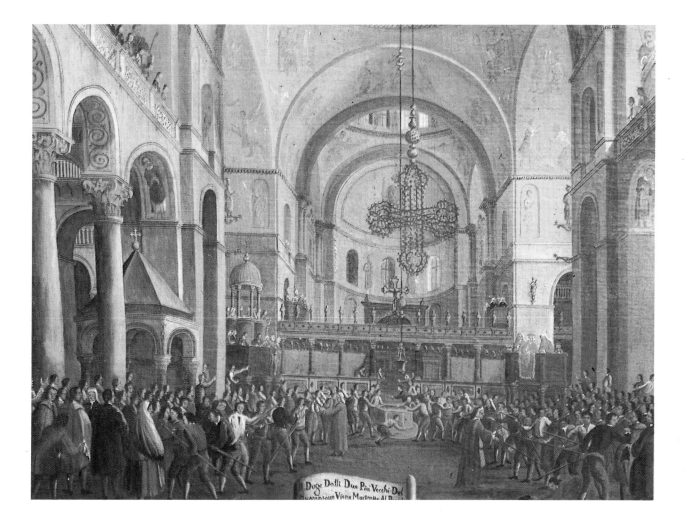

Doge Dolli Due Piu Vecchi Del
Quaran... un Viene Mostrato Al P...

In Vivaldi's time, political life in the prosperous republic of Venice was controlled by not more than fifty patrician families which were engaged in merchant shipping and inscribed in the *Libro d'Oro* (the "Golden Book"). The highest executive powers rested with the *doge*, a sort of duke and president, who was chosen by the Great Council. His activities were controlled by a Senate and later by the "Council of Ten."

The newly–chosen Doge (President) is presented to the people in the basilica of San Marco (Gabriele Bella, Venice, Pinacoteca Querini Stampalia).

The luxurious lifestyle led by the rich, aristocratic families of Venice in Vivaldi's time is splendidly illustrated in this painting: A Meal for Guests in the House of the Nanni–Mocenigo Family on Giudecca. *Giudecca is the long island to the south of the city (Venice, Museo del Settecento Veneziano di Ca' Rezzonico).*

Above: *The Ospedale della Pietà*
in a lithograph by A. Portio and A.
Dalla Via (Venice, Museo Correr).

A girl from one of the ospedali in
a lithograph by Vincenzo
Coronelli, from the "Ordinum
religiosorum in Ecclesia militanti,"
Venice, 1707 (Venice, Biblioteca
Nazionale Marciana).

According to his own account, within a year of being ordained Vivaldi no longer wished to celebrate mass because of physical complaints ("tightness of the chest") which pointed to "angina pectoris," asthmatic bronchitis, or a nervous disorder. It is also possible that Vivaldi was simulating illness – there is a story that he sometimes left the altar in order to quickly jot down a musical idea in the sacristy.... In any event he had become a priest against his own will, perhaps because of his mother's vow, or perhaps because in his day training for the priesthood was often the only possible way for a poor family to obtain free schooling.

Apparently musical education and, in Vivaldi's case, violin instruction were compulsory subjects, because a few months after his ordination as priest in 1703 he was named for the first time as violin teacher at the Ospedale della Pietà. The "ospedali" were typical Venetian institutions, orphanages where musical training went hand in hand with charity.

Until 1709, Vivaldi's appointment was renewed every year and again after 1711. Almost nothing is known of the intervening years – other than the fact that Vivaldi remained active as a composer – because in 1711 twelve concertos he had written were published in Amsterdam by the music publisher Estienne Roger under the title *L'Estro armonico* (Harmonic Inspiration).

Choirgirls from an ospedale singing in the "Procuratia Filarmonica fatta ai Duchi del Nord." A painting by Gabriele Bella (Venice, Pinacoteca Querini Stampalia).
Vivaldi was associated with the Ospedale della Pietà for a total of thirty years as a violin teacher, conductor, and composer without, as he himself said, "a single scandal," something which appears to have been an exception.

The title page of the Venetian publication of Vivaldi's first composition, the Sonate a tre opus 1 *of 1705, dedicated to Count Annibale Gambara (Bologna, Museo Bibliografico).*

VIOLINO PRIMO.

SVONATE DA CAMERA

A Trè due Violini, e Violone ò Cembalo

CONSACRATE

All' Illuſtriſſimo, & Eccelentiſſimo Signor Conte

ANNIBALE GAMBARA

NOBILE VENETO & c.

Dà D. Antonio Viualdi Muſico di Violino Profeſſore Veneto

OPERA PRIMA.

IN VENETIA. Da Gioſeppe Sala. M. D. CCV.

Si Vendono à S. Gio: Griſoſtimo All'Inſegna del Rè Dauid.

Foundlings, orphans, and illegitimate children were taken into the four Venetian ospedali. These concerned only girls. In addition to a normal education, the most gifted were also given musical tuition. They were called the "figlie di choro" (choirgirls), in which "choir" stood for musical education in the broadest sense. The ospedali had a long history; the oldest dated from 1346.

The intention was that the girls would marry someone from the middle classes, who could rest assured that his wife had received a good education, something which was a rarity in Venice at that time. What a prospective bridegroom could not be completely certain about, however, was his wife–to–be's virginity, since in the ospedali there were merry goings–on outside lesson hours!

Vivaldi's first published works were *twelve sonatas a tre* (1705), twelve sonatas dedicated to King Frederick IV of Denmark (1709), and the twelve concertos published in Amsterdam which have already been mentioned.

In Vivaldi's time, a composer who wished to obtain the favor of the public had to at least have a volume of Sonatas a tre printed and published at his own expense. These sonatas were written for two solo instruments, usually two violins, and a *basso continuo*, which could be played by cello or bassoon in combination with harpsichord or lute.

There were two types of *sonata a tre – da camera*, that is to say written in a style that resembled the one–tone dance music of that time and *da chiesa*, written in a more complex style derived from the many–voiced choral music of

the church. It was Vivaldi's older contemporary, Arcangelo Corelli, who had set the standard for these Sonatas a tre in his first published works.

In total, Vivaldi wrote some 90 sonatas, a form he apparently considered less important than the more complex *concerti*, of which he composed almost 500. He had his first sonatas and concertos printed in Amsterdam by Estienne Roger because Roger achieved much more legible results using new printing techniques. By doing this, Vivaldi hoped to sell more copies. Sometimes he sold them himself directly to friends and acquaintances, at the same time offering them violin lessons.

The Violin *and* The Harpsichord, *prints from the Gabinetto Armonico of Filippo Bonanni (Venice, Biblioteca Nazionale Marciana).*

Right: *The title page of* L'Estro
armonico *(Harmonic inspiration),
printed in Amsterdam. These concertos for strings, opus 3 (1711),
were enormously successful in
Vivaldi's time and later inspired –
among others – Johann Sebastian
Bach (above, Berlin, Archiv für
Kunst und Geschichte).*

Of the twelve concertos which together form the L'Estro armonico *four were written for solo violin, two for two violins, two for two violins and cello, one for four violins and three for four violins and cello.*
Opposite: The concert, *a painting by Pietro Longhi (Venice, Galleria dell'Accademia).*

In the baroque period it became the custom to number compositions in chronological order. "Opus 3 no. 5," for example, referred to a *group* of compositions from a certain period. The opus number (often shortened to "op.") "3" indicated the group referred to and the number "5" to the work within that group. This is the oldest form of cataloguing, and one which was mostly used by the composers themselves. But in many instances the sequence of the works of a composer was later changed, on the grounds of new insights or other criteria. When this occurred the author of the new catalogue gave a work a new number, next to the old number.

As far as Vivaldi is concerned, the scholar Antonio Fanna was the first to introduce a new classification. In his catalogue a composition was coded with the letter F (for Fanna), a Roman numeral that indicated the type of composition and an Arabic numeral that fixed the sequence. For example, "F I no. 3" meant Violin Voncerto, no. 3 and "F II no. 5" meant Viola Concerto, no. 5. A classification such as this is to be preferred particularly when there is some uncertainty about the true chronological order.

After Fanna a few other musicologists catalogued Vivaldi's oeuvre (Pincherle, Rinaldi), but since 1974 Peter Ryom's classification has been used (RV is abbreviated form of *Ryoms Verzeichnis*). His catalogue begins with the works for solo instruments and continuo (RV 1–108), then follow pieces for orchestra and concertos for solo instruments and orchestra

(RV 109–585) and the vocal compositions (RV 586–740). Finally, there are further numbers for other various categories (RV 741–750) and for recently discovered works (RV 751–780). At the back of this book there is a survey of Vivaldi's most important works, together with their RV numbers (pp. 76–80).

In the 17th century, various new forms of ensemble in small and large orchestral settings were created. One of these was the baroque

symphony, which should not be confused with the later symphonies by, for example, Haydn, Mozart, and Beethoven. The Baroque symphony emanated from the theater – people wanted a stage play (and in particular a musical stage play) preceded by a composition for instruments only. This introduction was given the name *sinfonia* in Italian and *ouverture* in French. The latter name was later used in the rest of Europe.

Opera Seria *(of the school of
Longhi, Milan, Museo Teatrale alla
Scala). At the beginning of such an
opera a "sinfonia" sounded.*

From the simplest form, a few introductory
solemn chords, came more complex forms with
the complete setting of a full orchestra and with
changes of tempo in the performance. In France
this sequence was slow–quick–slow, but in Italy
it was quick–slow–quick. Finally, the Italian *sinfonia avanti l'opera* broke free from the theater
and was no longer an introduction but a musical
form in its own right.

The *concerto grosso*, of which Vivaldi wrote
so many, was first designated as a specific Italian
instrumental genre in 1714 when Arcangelo
Corelli's *opus* 6 first appeared in print. Corelli
reverted to musical forms which had been used
by an earlier generation – 17th–century composers, including Alessandro Stradella and

The Piazza Maggiore in Bologna by Johannes Blaeu (Venice, Biblioteca Nazionale Marciana).

Giuseppe Torelli. In his day Torelli was the dominant figure in the musical life of Bologna, and Corelli also spent a fruitful time there.

Corelli split the orchestra into two parts, the *concerto grosso* or *tutti* (all) and the *concertino* or *soli*, each with its own *basso continuo*. The concertino consisted mostly of two violins and a cello and contrasted with the string orchestra. The basso continuo of this was usually entrusted to a keyboard instrument.

The result was a less rigid and more complex musical structure in which the solo parts also showed up to advantage compared to the rather static music of the Renaissance. (On page 25 the most important differences between Baroque and Renaissance music are given.)

View of Venice by Canaletto (Paris, Louvre).

IL CIMENTO DELL' ARMONIA
E DELL' INVENTIONE
Concerti
a 4 e 5
Consacrati
ALL' ILLUSTRISSIMO SIGNORE
*Il Signor Venceslao Conte di Marzin, Signore Ereditario
di Hohenelbe, Lomniz, Tschista, Krzinetz, Kaunitz, Doubek,
et Sowolusku, Cameriere Attuale, e Consigliere di*
S. M. C. C.
DA D. ANTONIO VIVALDI
*Maestro in Italia dell' Illustris.mo Signor Conte Sudetto,
Maestro de' Concerti del Pio Ospitale della Pietà in Venetia,
e Maestro di Capella dà Camera di S. A. S. il Signor
Principe Filippo Langravio d'Hassia Darmistath*
OPERA OTTAVA
Libro Primo

A AMSTERDAM
Spesa di MICHELE CARLO LE CENE
Libraro

*Sonetto Dimostrativo
Sopra il Concerto Intitolato La*
PRIMAVERA
DEL SIG.re D. ANTONIO VIVALDI

A *Giunt' è la Primavera e festosetti*
B *La Salutan gl' Augei con lieto canto,*
C *E i fonti allo Spirar de' Zeffiretti*
   Con dolce mormorio Scorrono intanto

D *Vengon' coprendo l'aer di nero amanto*
   E Lampi, e tuoni ad annuntiarla eletti

E *Indi tacendo questi, gl' Augelletti;*
   Tornan' di nuovo allor canoro incanto:

F *E quindi Sul fiorito ameno prato*
   Al caro mormorio di fronde e piante
   Dorme 'l Caprar col fido can' à lato.

G *Di pastoral Zampogna al Suon festante*
   Danzan Ninfe e Pastor nel tetto amato
   Di primavera all'apparir brillante.

Concerning instrumental work, according to the latest research Antonio Vivaldi wrote a total of 90 sonatas, 478 concertos, and 14 symphonies. His most important collection is probably Il cimento dell'armonia e dell'invenzione, opus 8, published by La Cène in Amsterdam in 1725.
Above left: The title page (Bologna, Civico Museo Bibliografico).
The first four concertos of this collection are known as I quattro stagioni (The Four Seasons). Other concertos also received names, such as the fifth: La tempesta di mare (Storm at Sea), the sixth: Il piacere (Pleasure) and the tenth: La caccia (The Hunt). These seven concertos are superior examples of descriptive music in which physical phenomena (storm, rain, etc.) are imitated by the instruments. Each part of The Four Seasons is preceded by a sonnet, most probably by Vivaldi's own hand. In the margin Vivaldi put letters of the alphabet which correspond with letters in the score in order to clarify the relationship between the music and the text.
Above right: the "Sonnetto dimostrativo," which precedes Spring of The Four Seasons (Bologna, Civico Museo Bibliografico).
(See pages 48–53 for an extended schema of The Four Seasons.)

The most significant differences between the music of the Renaissance (ca. 1500 – 1650) and of the Baroque (1650 – 1750).

Renaissance	Baroque
Monomorphic style	Complex style
All voices of equal importance	The two extreme voices (high and low) are the most important
Little developed diatonic melody without chromatics	Rich diatonic and chromatic melody
Harmony based on intervals	Harmony based on chords
The use of the human voice and of the instruments is free, they are mutually interchangeable	The use of the human voice and the instruments is strictly regulated, even when they are interchangeable

Left: *The Ospedale degli Incurabili in a lithograph by Luca Carlevarijs from the early 18th century.*

Right: *The Ospedale dei Mendicanti, in a lithograph by Luca Carlevarijs from the beginning of the 18th century (Venice, Museo Correr).*

View of Venice, a painting by Canaletto (Vienna, Kunsthistorisches Museum).

In the first thirty years of the 18th century, when Vivaldi was active in Venice, musical life there was determined by three types of institutions. To begin with, there was the San Marco orchestra, the most distinguished and most official institution. Then there were the four ospedali: della Pietà – to which Vivaldi was attached and which enjoyed the greatest prestige – Ospedaletto, degli Incurabili, and dei Mendicanti. Finally, there were the numerous opera theaters of which the first, the San Cassiano, had opened as early as 1580.

Moreover what were known as *accademie*, musical evenings given by aristocratic families for their guests, were held in private houses. Great crowds of people collected outside the "palazzi" in order to catch a trace of the music.

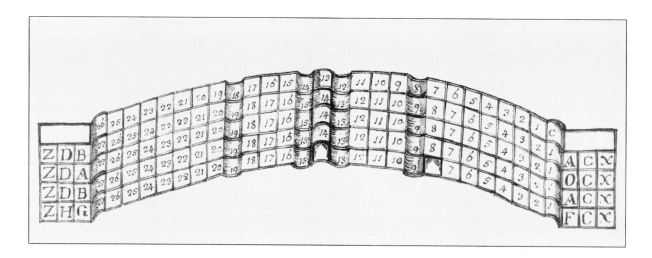

Above: *Diagram of the boxes of the Teatro Sant' Angelo in the second half of the 18th century. Vivaldi sometimes acted as impresario for this opera theater (Venice, Museo Correr).*

Right: *Title page of* Orlando finto pazzo, *a musical drama by Vivaldi written in 1714 and performed in the Teatro Sant' Angelo.*

Between 1709 and 1711 Vivaldi was not attached to the Ospedale della Pietà. Perhaps in this period he was already working with the Teatro Sant' Angelo, an opera theater. After 1711, he was occasionally given leave to travel and to give concerts in other Italian cities and abroad. Nonetheless, he remained firmly attached to the ospedale until 1740, a year before his death.

His most important tasks were giving violin tuition and composing various types of music, including church music. Furthermore, he had to acquire music from other composers for the numerous concerts which were given in the ospedale.

In around 1750, in the Ospedale della Pietà there were eighteen female choristers, eight female players of stringed instruments, two organists, two solo female choristers, a lady

In 1716, Vivaldi also collaborated with the Teatro San Moisè which performed his opera La Costanza trionfante degli Amori e degli Odii *for the carnival of that year.*
Left: *View of the Teatro San Moisè on the Grand Canal (Venice, Museo Correr).*

Below: *The title page of* Juditha Triumphans, *Vivaldi's first big oratorio, 1716.*

teacher for the instruments, and one for the choir and fourteen pupils. Famous outside teachers were brought in to instruct the oldest girls who, in their turn, gave lessons to the younger pupils. Virtuosi were also brought in from outside for the playing of instruments – such as the trumpet – which were not suitable for girls.

It is curious that the parts for the lower voices in the choir (tenor and bass) were also sung by the girls: in the archives of the ospedale they are registered, for example, as "Paolina del tenor" and "Anneta del basso." In fact, all the music students excelled so well that they were more admired than many well–known virtuosi. Together they formed a professional choir and orchestra for which Vivaldi organized concerts in Venice and the surrounding area. Music lovers came from far and wide, even from abroad.

JUDITHA TRIUMPHANS
DEVICTA HOLOFERNIS BARBARIE
Sacrum Militare Oratorium
HISCE BELLI TEMPORIBUS
A Psalentium Virginum Choro
IN TEMPLO PIETATIS CANENDUM
JACOBI CASSETTI EQ,
METRICE' VOTIS EXPRESSVM.
Piissimis ipsius Orphanodochii PRÆSI-
DENTIBVS ac GUBERNATORIBUS
submissè Dicatum .
MUSICE' EXPRESSUM
Ab Admod. Riv. D.
ANTONIO VIVALDI

VENETIIS . MDCCXVI.
Apud Bartholomæum Occhium, sub signo S. Dominici.
SVPERIORVM PERMISSV.

*The chamber music which Vivaldi and his contemporaries wrote was esteemed throughout Europe and was also used to instruct a growing flock of musical amateurs.
Above:* The Music Lesson *by Matthijs Nalveu (Bourg–en–Bresse, Musée de l'Ain).*

It is certain that on April 30th. 1713, Vivaldi was given a month's leave from the Ospedale della Pietà in order to stage his first opera, *Ottone in villa*, in Vicenza. In the 1713–1714 season he was once again attached to the Teatro Sant' Angelo, where he made the work *Orlando furioso*, by Giovanni Alberto Rostori (1692–1753) suitable for performance.

In addition he wrote his own "musical drama" *Orlando finto pazzo* for the Teatro Sant' Angelo. In 1715, Vivaldi was even known to be a partner in the opera theater, where he also performed as a solo violinist. This continued until 1718.

A contemporay of Vivaldi, J. F. A. von Uffenbach, who attended one of his concerts, wrote: "Vivaldi played a wonderful 'solo' and finished off with an improvised cadenza which amazed me. It is impossible that such a cadenza

Lady at the Spinet, *a 17th–century painting by Godert de Wedig (Cologne, Museum Wallraf–Richartz).*

has ever been played before or shall ever be played again. His fingers came so close to the bridge that there was scarcely room for the bow. He did this on all four strings, with imitations and with a marvellous speed that astounded everyone."

As far as his theatrical activities were concerned, the end of 1716 was a high point for Vivaldi. In November, he managed to have the Ospedale della Pietà perform his first great oratorio, *Juditha Triumphans devicta Holofernis barbarie*. This work was an allegorical description of the victory of the Venetians (the Christians) over the Turks (the barbarians) in August 1716.

Vivaldi's famous collection of 12
concertos, opus 3, which he entitl-
ed L'Estro armonico (Harmonic
Inspiration), is one of the
best–known examples of Italian
baroque music, elegantly con-
structed music which sparkles with
new musical ideas.
Right: Apollo and the Muses by
Marten de Vos (Brussels,
Koninklijk Museum voor de
Schone Kunsten).

MVSÆ·LOCO
BELLI

F·MD·VOS

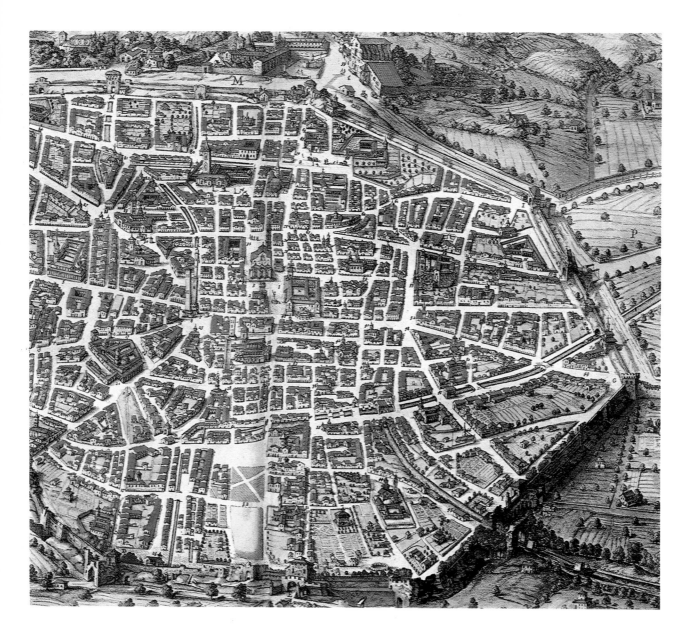

Above: *A 17th–century view of the city of Bologna from an atlas by the cartographer Johannes Blaeu (Venice, Biblioteca Nazionale Marciana).*

Above left: *Arcangelo Corelli in a contemporary etching (Venice, Museo Correr).*

Above right: *Portrait of the French writer Jean–Jacques Rousseau by Jean–Edouard Lacretelle (Versailles, Musée du Château).*

As has already been mentioned, the composer Arcangelo Corelli (1653–1713) was a famous contemporay of Vivaldi. When he had just turned thirteen, Corelli's life in Bologna was already completely dominated by music. Four years later, he had already been accepted as a member of the local Accademia Filarmonica. Thanks to the protection of Cardinal Pietro Ottoboni, Corelli was able to dedicate himself completely to music. In a short time he became a symbol of the struggle for artistic perfection in Italian music.

In his own time, Corelli enjoyed more prestige than his colleagues and some biographers explain this by pointing to a journey that he was said to have made through France, a journey that enriched his musical knowledge enormously. There are indications that he did indeed undertake such a journey, as certain passages in *Letter on French Music* by Jean–Jacques Rousseau suggest. The French writer claimed that it was the French composer Lully, driven by jealousy, who finally forced Corelli to leave France.

The Venetian Teatro San Giovanni
Grisostomo, governed by the
Grimani family, in an etching by
Vincenzo Coronelli (Venice, Museo
Correr).

At the end of 1717 Vivaldi moved to Mantua for two years in order to take up his post as Chamber Kapellmeister at the court of Landgrave Philips van Hessen–Darmstadt. His task there was to to provide operas, cantatas, and perhaps concert music, too. His opera *Armida* had already been performed earlier in Mantua and in 1719 *Teuzzone* and *Tito Manlio* followed. On the score of the latter are the words: "music by Vivaldi, made in 5 days." Furthermore, in 1720 *La Candace o siano Li veri amici* was performed.

In 1720, Vivaldi returned to Venice where he again staged new operas written by himself in the Teatro Sant' Angelo. This was a period in his life in which important events took place. To begin with, in Mantua he had made the acquaintance of the singer Anna Giraud (or Girò), and she had moved in to live with him. Vivaldi maintained that she was no more than a housekeeper

and good friend, just like Anna's sister, Paolina, who also shared his house.

In his *Mémoires*, the Italian playwright Carlo Goldoni gave the following portrait of Vivaldi and Giraud: "This priest, an excellent violinist but a mediocre composer, has trained Miss Giraud to be a singer. She was young, born in Venice, but the daughter of a French wigmaker. She was not beautiful, though she was elegant, small in stature, with beautiful eyes and a fascinating mouth. She had a small voice, but many languages in which to harangue." Vivaldi stayed together with her until his death.

In the same period he had to contend with a stringent attack on his work. In 1720 in Venice the aristocratic jurist and amateur composer Benedetto Marcello (1686–1739) published the polemic text *Il teatro alla moda*. It was a reactionary and jealous, but also witty, attack on "modern" Italian opera of the time. Opera in

Bullfight in the Campo San Polo *by Joseph Heinz (Venice, Museo Correr).*

which – also by Vivaldi – emphasis was laid on the use of the voice as an instrument, virtuosity, a pure sound, and an obvious construction; matters which were probably over the head of the old–fashioned Marcello.

The opera theaters in Venice were the greatest attractions in the city in the 17th and 18th centuries. As instrumental music was linked to the ospedali, so were operas performed in the many theaters where people could also gamble – this often yielded a better return!

The San Giovanni Grisostomo theater was regared as the most luxurious in the city. It was the custom – as it was in the rest of Europe – that an aristocratic family looked after a theater financially, sometimes organized performances or left them in the hands of an impresario such as Vivaldi. The San Giovanni Grisostomo theater was controlled by the Grimani family.

From 17th– and 18th–century paintings and other depictions of life in Venice, it appears that people were preoccupied with everything that could embellish life and make it more pleasant. Besides concerts and operas, all sorts of festive spectacles, such as dance competitions, masked balls, bullfights, and open–air performances, were organized both indoors and out.

Strolling on San Marco Square on the occasion of the "Festa della Sensa." This festival was celebrated on Ascension Day and was combined with an old ceremony "Marriage to the Sea": The Doge (President) threw a ring into the waves in order to commemorate the symbolic marriage between Venice and the sea.

Celebration in the Piazza Santa Croce in Florence in an anonymous 18th–century painting (Nancy, Musée Historique Lorrain).

After 1718 Vivaldi frequently stayed in other Italian cities when his works were being performed there. He often conducted himself, or functioned as solo violinist. After his debut opera, *Ottone in villa* in 1713 in Vicenza, *Scanderberg* was one of the first operas by Vivaldi not to be performed in a Venetian theater. This work was premiered in the Teatro della Pergola in Florence.

The "pastoral drama" *La Silvia* was performed in Milan in 1721, and in 1723 and 1724 Vivaldi was in Rome where various operas of his were staged. He himself referred in a letter to the three seasons he spent in Rome, but it is still not clear when the third stay took place.

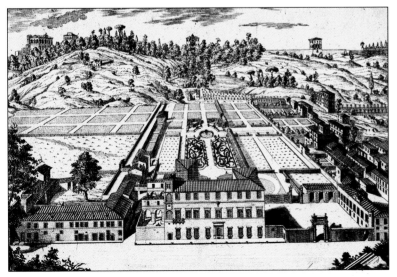

Above: *A performance of* La Sena
Festeggiante *in a reconstruction by
Pannini (Paris, Louvre).*

Left: *A view of the Palazzo Riario
in Rome, which Christina of
Sweden had made her residence in
the 1680s. Here she organized
musical events attended by composers such as Corelli and Scarlatti
(Roma, Gabinetto Nazionale delle
Stampe).*

Vivaldi also wrote works on commission from foreign rulers, such as the French king, Louis XV – the serenade *La Sena Festeggiante* (Festival on the Seine), for example. This work cannot be dated precisely, but it was certainly written after 1720.

In Rome Vivaldi found a patron in the person of Cardinal Pietro Ottoboni, a great music lover, who earlier had been the Maecenas (patron) of Arcangelo Corelli. And if we can believe Vivaldi himself, the Pope asked him to come and play the violin for him at a private audience.

Tangible evidence of Vivaldi's stay in Rome has survived in the form of the only authentic, drawn from life, portrait of the composer. This caricature (see page 10) was drawn by the famous artist Pier Leone Ghezzi, who captured Roman society of that time in his lively style of drawing.

In the 1660's, musical life in Rome had been enormously stimulated by the presence of Christina of Sweden in the city. The "Pallas of the North," as she was called, abdicated from the Swedish throne in 1654. A few years later she moved to Rome and took up residence in the Palazzo Riario. There she organized musical events that were attended by composers such as Corelli and Scarlatti. Other composers, too, such as Geminiani and Händel worked in Rome for periods of time. Like them, Vivaldi profited from the favorable cultural climate in the city.

The "Trinità dei Monti" church in Rome by Gaspare van Wittel (Rome, Palazzo Barberini).

Despite his stay in Rome and other cities, Vivaldi remained in the service of the Ospedale della Pietà, which nominated him "Maestro di concerti." He only had to send two concertos per month to Venice (transport costs were to the account of the client) and he received a ducat per concerto. His presence was never required. He also remained director of the Teatro Sant' Angelo, as he did in the 1726, 1727, and 1728 seasons. The attack by Marcello on the new form of opera theater had been forgotten, and Vivaldi's method of working had conquered the whole of Italy and Europe. Nevertheless, this fashion would also disappear, and with it the interest in Vivaldi's operas and even his instrumental music.

Between 1725 and 1728 some eight operas were premiered in Venice and Florence. Abbot

Conti wrote of his contemporary, Vivaldi: "In less than three months Vivaldi has composed three operas, two for Venice and a third for Florence; the last has given something of a boost to the name of the theater of that city and he has earned a great deal of money."

During these years Vivaldi was also extremely active in the field of concertos. In 1725 the publication *Il Cimento dell'Armonia e dell'Invenzione* (The trial of harmony and invention), opus 8, appeared in Amsterdam. This consisted of twelve concertos, seven of which were descriptive: *The Four Seasons, Storm at Sea, Pleasure* and *The Hunt*. Vivaldi transformed the tradition of descriptive music into a typically Italian musical style with its unmistakable timbre in which the strings play a big role.

These concertos were enormously successful, particularly in France. In the second half of the 18th century there even appeared remarkable adaptations of *Spring*. Michel Corrette (1709–1795) based his motet *Laudate Dominum de coelis* of 1765 on Vivaldi's concerto and, in 1775, Jean–Jacques Rousseau reworked it into a version for solo flute.

King Louis XV was also mad about this concerto and ordered it to be performed at the most unexpected moments. Moreover, Vivaldi received various commissions for compositions from the court at Versailles.

Large Orchestra, *detail from a painting by Gabriele Bella (Venice, Galleria Querini Stampalia). Compared to Renaissance music,* baroque music in Vivaldi's time developed enormously. The concerto grosso, for large orchestra, was a great step forwards.

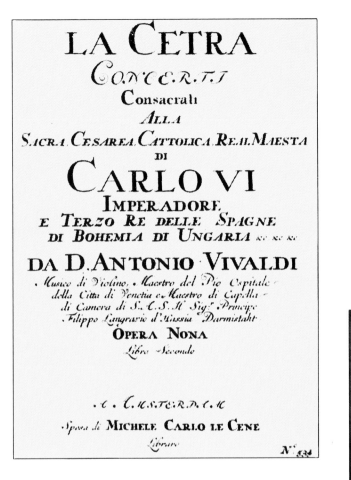

Besides Louis XV of France, Vivaldi was also admired by Emperor Charles VI, depicted below in a portrait by Johann Kupetzky (Vienna, Historisches Museum der Stadt). He had probably met the emperor in Trieste in 1728. "The Emperor has given Vivaldi much money, a chain and a gold medal... and has made him a knight," can be read in the Abbot Conti's correspondence, and: "The Emperor has spoken for a long time with Vivaldi about music and it is said that in fifteen days he has discussed more with him than he has in two years with his ministers..."

Above: *The title page of the collection of concertos named* La Cetra *(The Zither), opus 9, with a dedication to Emperor Charles VI.*

THE FOUR SEASONS

Vivaldi's best–known work consists of four concertos each of which was inspired by a season of the year and each of which have the three–part form quick–slow–quick, the composer's favorite method of composition. In order to make the performance of the work more attractive to the public, Vivaldi added four sonnets, probably written by himself, which

SPRING					
Progress	Stage		Performers	Theme	Tempi
ALLEGRO	1.		tutti	Introductory	forte
	2.				piano
	1.	Spring has arrived		A (spring)	forte
	4.				piano
	5.	and the birds greet her festively with joyous song	violin solo violins	B	forte
	6.		tutti	A	
	7.	as streamlets murmer softly beneath her balmy breeze.		C	piano
	8.			A	forte
	9.	Thunder and lighting have been chosen to announce her coming, throwing an ink–black mantle across the heavens.		D A minor	mezzoforte
	10.				
	11.	And then, when they fall silent, the birds return with charming song.	violins	E	piano
	12.		tutti	A	forte
	13.		violin solo	F	piano
	14.		tutti	A	forte
	15.				piano
LARGO	1.	And now upon the lovely flowering heather, beneath the soft rustle of leafy branches, the shepherd sleeps, his faithful dog beside him.	violin solo violins and viola	G	pianissimo sempre
ALLEGRO Pastorale	1.	To the festive sound of rustic bagpipes	tutti	H	forte
	2.				piano
	3.	nymphs dance with the shepherd		I	forte
	4.				piano
	5.	in honor of the spring in all her splendor.	violin solo	L	forte
	6.		tutti	H	
	7.			M	
	8.		violins	(series)	piano
	9.		tutti	H	forte
	10.			(interim)	piano
	11.		violin solo	(continuation)	
	12.		tutti	H	forte
	13.			repetition of the end	piano

functioned as the program. In the schema which follows, the words of the sonnets are set beside the musical moments to which they belong, in order to provide the reader/listener with an insight into the construction of the music.
The four concertos are dedicated to Count Wenceslaus di Marzin and were probably played for the first time by the nobleman's private orchestra, with Vivaldi himself as conductor.
The composer attempted to reflect the phenomena of nature in the music. This was something often attempted in his time, but his interpretations are among the most charming in baroque music.

Right: *A detail from* Concert in the Open Air *by Ludovico Pozzoserrato (Treviso, Museo Civico).*

SUMMER					
Progress	Stage		Performers	Theme	Tempi
ALLEGRO NON MOLTO	1.	In this tedious season of the blazing sun men and flocks are sweltering and pines are seared	tutti	A	pianissimo
	2.	the cuckoo regains its voice,	violin solo	B	piano
	3.	repetition of the end	tutti		forte
	4.	and soon the turtle dove	violin solo	C	piano
	5.	and finch begin to sweetly sing.		D	
	6.	The sweet breeze of summer blows,	tutti	E	
	7.	but suddenly the contentious north wind elbows these soft winds aside;		F	forte
	8.	then weeps the shepherd, for he fears	violin solo	G	piano
	9.	the violence of the cold wind and what it may betide.	tutti	H	forte
ADAGIO	1.	His tired limbs are robbed of rest	violins	I	piano
	2.	by fear of lightning and rude thunder's	tutti	L	forte
	3.	roar, and angry swarms of flies	violins	M	piano
	4.	both great and small.	tutti		
PRESTO passionate summer tempo	1.	Alas, his greatest fears are confirmed;	tutti	N	forte
	2.	the heavens growl and flash and hailstones			
	3.	pound the ripened, lofty corn.			

AUTUMN				
Progress	Stage	Performers	Theme	Tempi
ALLEGRO The peasant boys' song and dance	1. The peasants celebrate with song and dance	tutti	A	forte
	2. their happiness at harvest safely home,			piano
	3.	violin solo		
	4.	tutti	A completed	forte
	5. and for many who yield to Bacchus' charms	violin solo	B	
	6.	tutti	A	
	7.	violin solo	C	piano
	8.	tutti	A	forte
	9. their pleasure ends in sleep.		D	piano
	10.		A	forte
ADAGIO The drunkards sleep	1. The balmy weather in which men all delight, and the summons of the season to the great enjoyment of their sweet repose make everyone forget singing and dancing	tutti	E	piano
ALLEGRO The hunt	1. At new day's dawn the hunters	tutti	F	forte
	2. sally forth with horns and guns and dogs;		G	
	3.			piano
	4.			forte
	5.			piano
	6.		F	forte
	7.			piano
	8.		G	
	9.		F	forte
	10.	violin solo	H	
	11.	tutti	F	
	12. the prey takes to its heels and they pursue its trail.	violin solo	I	
	13. Shocked and half paralysed by din of dogs and guns,	tutti	L	
	14.	violin solo	M	
	15.	tutti	F	
	16.	violin solo	N	mezzoforte
	17.	tutti	F	forte
	18. and wounded, wearily it attempts to flee	violin solo	P	mezzoforte
	19. but, stricken, dies.	tutti		
	20.		G	forte
	21.			piano
	22.		F	forte

Right: *Autumn, one of the four seasons on a carpet, woven in the Gobelin workshop of S. Barbara, after sketches by Jacopo Amigoni (Madrid, Royal Palace).*

WINTER				
Progress	Stage	Performers	Theme	Tempi
ALLEGRO NON MOLTO	1. Chilled and shivering in the icy snow	tutti	A	forte
	2. in powerful gusts of bitter wind,	violin solo	B	
	3. running, ever stamping feet	tutti	C	
	4.	violin solo	D	
	5.	tutti	E	mezzoforte
	6. teeth chattering		F	piano
	7. because of the bitter chill.		C	forte
LARGO	1. To pass the days before the fire, happy and content, while outside rain drenches wellnigh all.	violin solo and tutti	G	mezzoforte forte
ALLEGRO	1. To walk across the ice with tardy tread,	violin solo	H	mezzoforte
	2. moving carefully for fear of falling.	tutti	I	piano
	3. Run, slip, fall to the ground,		L	forte
	4. rise, hasten once again across the ice	violin solo and tutti	M	mezzoforte
	5. until it breaks and drifts away;	tutti	N	forte
	6.	violin solo		
	7. to hear how from out their iron–clad gates	tutti	O	piano
	8. Scirocco, Borea and all the other winds rush to the fray.	violin solo	P	forte
	9. That is the winter; and such are its delights.	tutti	Q	

The original Italian sonnets from The Four Seasons

LA PRIMAVERA

Giunt'è la primavera e festosetti
la salutan gl'augei con lieto canto,
e i fonti allo spirar de' zeffiretti
con dolce mormorio scorrono intanto.

Vengon' coprendo l'aer di nero ammanto
e lampi e tuoni ad annunziarla eletti;
indi tacendo questi, gl'augelletti
tornan di nuovo al lor canoro incanto.

E quindi sul fiorito ameno prato
al caro mormorio di fronde e piante
dorme 'l caprai col fido can' a lato.

Di pastoral zampogna al suon festante
danzan nimfe e pastor nel tetto amato
di primavera all'apparir brillante.

L'ESTATE

Sotto dura staggion dal sole accesa
langue l'huom, langue 'l gregge ed arde il pino,
scioglie il cucco la voce, e tosto intesa
canta la tortorella e 'l gardellino.

Zeffiro dolce spira, ma contesa
muove Borea improvvisa al suo vicino;
e piange il pastorel, perché sospesa
teme fiera borasca e 'l suo destino.
Toglie alle membra lasse il suo riposo
il timor de' lampi, e tuoni fieri
e de mosche e mosconi il stuol furioso!

Ah, che purtroppo i suoi timor son veri;
tuona e fulmina il ciel e grandinoso
tronca il capo alle spiche e a' grani alteri.

L'AUTUNNO

Celebra il villanel con balli e canti
del felice raccolto il bel piacere,
e del liquor di Bacco accesi tanti
finiscono col sonno il lor godere.

Fa ch'ognuno tralasci e balli e canti
l'aria che temperata da piacere
e la staggion che invita tanti e tanti
d'un dolcissimo sonno al bel godere.

I cacciator alla nov'alba a caccia
con corni, schioppi e cani escono fuore;
fugge la belva e seguono la traccia.

Già sbigottita e lassa al gran rumore
de' schioppi e cani, ferita minaccia
languida di fuggir, ma oppressa muore.

L'INVERNO

Agghiacciato tremar tra nevi algenti
al severo spirar d'orrido vento,
correr battendo i piedi ogni momento
e per soverchio gel batter i denti;

passar al foco i di quieti e contenti
mentre la pioggia fuor bagna ben cento.
Camminar sopra 'l ghiaccio, e a passo lento
per timor di cader girsene intenti.

Gir forte, sdrucciolar, cader a terra,
di nuovo ir sopra 'l ghiaccio e correr forte
sin ch'il ghiaccio si rompe e si disserra;

sentir uscir dalle ferrate porte
Sirocco, Borea e tutti i venti in guerra.
Quest'è l'inverno, ma tal che gioia apporte.

The freezing of the lagoon in 1706 by Gabriele Bella (Venice, Galleria Querini Stampalia).

Rowing regatta on the Grand
Canal *by Gabriele Bella (Vencie,
Galleria Querini Stampalia).*

Vivaldi continued to write and perform operas
– almost on a production line. In 1727 *Siroe, re
di Persia* was performed in the city of Reggio
Emilia. This opera was the first by Vivaldi which
had a libretto by Pietro Metastasio (actually
Pietro Trapassi (1698–1782). This famous man
of letters, composer, and singer, stamped his
mark on opera life in Italy for a long time. After
his enormous success in 1724 with the libretto
of *Didone abandonnata* (music by Domenico
Sarro) he had become a beacon for the new
generation of opera composers from the whole
of Europe.

Florence, Treviso, and Livorno were other
cities in which Vivaldi was active from 1727 to
1729.

In the years 1729–1730, the *Six Concertos,
opus 10* were printed in Amsterdam. In these
concertos the flute is given a major role as a solo
instrument for the first time. At the beginning of

the 18th century the recorder and the (wooden) flute (also known as "traverso") were both equally loved by musicians and composers. Then a collection of flute concertos by the French composer Joseph Bodin de Boismortier (1689-1755) appeared, and with the publication of Vivaldi's *opus* 10 the flute clearly began to become more popular than the recorder. Finally, Johann Joachim Quantz (1697–1773), a great flautist in the service of Frederick the Great, King of Prussia, ensured that the flute definitively prevailed. He wrote an enormous amount of music for the instrument, and in 1752 he wrote a famous textbook.

In 1729, Vivaldi's father was still alive and in service with the orchestra of San Marco Basilica. On September 30th of that year, he requested a year's leave in order to accompany one of his sons to "Germania." This probably concerned a journey Vivaldi, his father, and Anna Giraud made to Vienna and, in 1730, to Prague.

Above left: The flute, *illustration from* Il gabinetto armonico *by Filippo Bonanni (Venice, Biblioteca Nazionale Marciana).*

In May 1727, the opera Siroe, King of Persia, *Vivaldi's first opera with a libretto by Pietro Metastasio, and shown above in a contemporary etching, was premiered at the theater of Reggio Emilia (Venice, Biblioteca Nazionale Marciana).*

In the music–loving city of Prague (half a century later Mozart would celebrate his first operatic triumphs there) Vivaldi met a Venetian opera company which between 1724 and 1734 staged some sixty operas in the theater of Count Franz Anton von Sporck. In the 1730–1731 season, two new operas by Vivaldi were premiered there after the previous season had closed with his opera *Farnace*, a work the composer often used as his showpiece.

Unfortunately, the music of these two new operas, *Argippo* and *Alvilda regina dei Goti*, has not survived. In Turin, however, can be found the manuscripts of two sonatas and a lute concerto with the dedication "Per Sua Eccellenza Signor Conte Wrttbij." The music is written on differ-ent manuscript paper than Vivaldi normally used, and the dedication is to a member of the Prague aristocracy, an official to the emperor

and a great music lover. This is one of the indirect pieces of evidence of Vivaldi's presence in Prague.

At the end of 1731, Vivaldi returned to Venice, but at the beginning of 1732 he left again for Mantua and Verona. In Mantua, Vivaldi's opera *Semiramide* was performed and in Verona, on the occasion of the opening of the new Teatro Filarmonico, *La fida Ninfa*, with a libretto by the Veronese poet and man of letters, Scipione Maffei, was staged.

After his stay in Prague, Vivaldi concentrated mainly on operas. No further collections of instrumental music were published other than the sonatas of *Il Pastor fido*, which are not by Vivaldi, and the cello sonatas. This concerns a collection which is probably *opus* 14 and which was printed in Paris rather than in Amsterdam.

Above: *The interior of the Teatro Filarmonico in Verona during a rehearsal of Vivaldi's opera* La fida Ninfa.
right: *Portrait of the Veronese poet and littérateur, Scipione Maffei.*

Vivaldi continued to *write* instrumental music, although it was only to sell the manuscripts to private persons or to the Ospedale della Pietà, which after 1735 paid him a fixed honorarium of 100 ducats a year. In 1733 he met the English traveler, Edward Holdsworth, who had been commissioned to purchase a few of Vivaldi's compositions for the man of letters, Charles Jennens, author of texts for oratorios by Händel. Holdsworth wrote to Jennens: "I spoke with your friend Vivaldi today. He told me that he had decided to publish no more concertos because otherwise he can no longer sell his handwritten compositions. He earns more with these, he said, and since he charges one guinea per piece, that must be true if he finds a goodly number of buyers.

Il Ridotto, *a painting by Pietro Longhi (Venice, Museo Correr). "Il Ridotto" was a public gambling house in the Palazzo Dandolo, opened in 1683. Every Venetian was allowed inside, as long as they were masked. After the closure of Il Ridotto in 1774, on the order of the Council of Ten, more than a hundred illegal private gambling dens came into being.*

"Perhaps you should deal with him yourself or you should come here to look for something you like, but I would rather not take the risk of choosing something for you at that price."

Because Vivaldi was famous throughout the whole of Europe, he could afford to ask high prices for his music. Furthermore, he worked quickly. The French civil servant, Charles de Brosses, heard him boast that he "could compose all the parts of a concerto faster than a copyist could write them out."

Vivaldi also had pupils, who received instructions from him as to how they should perform the music they had just bought. These included Kapellmeisters from various German courts and also, for example, the Czech composer Jan Dismas Zelenka, who has only recently been recognized as one of the most important representatives of late Bohemian–German baroque music.

Left: *Apostolo Zeno, librettist of the opera* Griselda.

Above: *Title page of the libretto, adapted by Carlo Goldoni.*

In the 1733, 1734, and 1735 seasons, new operas by Vivaldi were performed in Venice and Verona, including *L'Olimpiade* in Venice. This was the first of Vivaldi's operas to be rediscovered in this century, and it was performed in Sienna in 1939 during the concert which would once again arouse interest in the composer.

The first collaboration between Vivaldi and the playwright Carlo Goldoni came about in the preparations for the opera *Griselda*, which was premiered on Ascension Day 1735, in the Teatro Grimani in Venice. Goldoni's memoirs tell us that at first Vivaldi treated the then 28–year–old

writer arrogantly and in fact had little faith in his abilities. But after Goldoni had reworked the libretto for the opera, which had been written by Apostolo Zeno, the composer was full of praise: "... he embraced me once again, complimented me, I am his Friend, his Poet, his Confidant, and it remained so. I had killed off Zeno's Drama exactly as he had wanted."

This collaboration was quickly followed by the comic heroic opera *Aristide*, which was performed in the autumn in another of the Grimani family's theaters, the San Samuele theater.

It is not clear why, after 1736, Vivaldi had set his mind on directing an opera season in the city of Ferrara. The project would eventually be unsuccessful. The course of events can be charted exactly from an extensive exchange of correspondence with a nobleman of that city, the Marquis Guido d'Aragona Bentivoglio. Thirteen of Vivaldi's letters, written between November 3, 1736 and January 2, 1739, have survived.

Vivaldi had met Bentivoglio in Rome in 1723. The aristocrat was a good amateur mandolin player and perhaps some of Vivaldi's mandolin concertos were written specially for him. Furthermore, members of the Bentivoglio family

had been known as patrons of music in their city since the 16th century. Guido also concerned himself with the organization of operatic performances in Ferrara and invited Vivaldi, who he himself had recommended, to be both impresario and musical director, a double function he had performed so successfully in Venice.

After much bickering about payment, it was agreed that Vivaldi would stage an opera in Ferrara in late 1737, but as emerges from a famous letter to Bentivoglio, dated November 16, 1736, Vivaldi's relationship with the singer Anna Giraud undid him, besides the fact that he no longer celebrated mass. Cardinal Tommaso

Letter from Vivaldi to the Marquis Bentivoglio, dated December 26, 1736.

Ruffo, Archbishop of Ferrara, had just begun a campaign to combat the moral decline among the clergy, and it was he who forbade Vivaldi to come to Ferrara.

In his letter Vivaldi complained: "After so many intrigues and so much effort the opera in Ferrara is now dead and gone. Today Monsignor, the Apostolic Nuncio, summoned me and in the name of His Eminence Ruffo forbade me to go to Ferrara and put on the opera, and this because as a servant of the church I no longer say Mass and am a friend of the singer Girò. You can imagine what a state I am in after such a blow. For this opera I have taken commitments for six thousand ducats on my shoulders and I have already spent more than a hundred.

Cardinal Francesco Grimani, member of the powerful Grimani family, owner of the theaters of San Samuele and San Giovanni Grisostomo in Venice. The cardinal played an important role in the management of the theaters and in the performances of Vivaldi's operas.

It is impossible to do the opera without Girò because nowhere will we find such a prima donna. I cannot do the opera without myself because I will not entrust such a large sum of money to other hands. On the other hand I must fulfill my commitments and therefore the disaster is incalculable. What grieves me the most is that His Eminence Ruffo tarnishes the reputation of these poor ladies, something the world has never done. For fourteen years the three of us have visited very many cities in Europe and everywhere they were admired for their probity, particularly in Ferrara, I might say. Every eight days they make their confession...

*Cardinal Tommaso Ruffo,
Archbishop of Ferrara, in an
etching by Andrea Bolzoni
(Ferrara, Biblioteca Comunale
Ariostea).*

I have not celebrated Mass for twenty–five years and I shall never do so again, not because I am too old or because I am forbidden to, as you may inform His Eminence, but of my own free choice and because since birth I have suffered from a complaint which makes me short of breath. When I had just been ordained a priest I celebrated Mass for a year or so and then no more, because three times I had to leave the altar without completing Mass due to this same complaint. Therefore I almost never leave my house and only travel by gondola or coach because I cannot walk because of the complaint in my chest or the tightness of my chest. No gentleman of standing invites me to his home, even our own Count, because all of them know of my infirmity. Immediately after the midday meal I can usually move about, but never on foot. That is the reason I no longer celebrate Mass..."

The lamentation goes on for paragraphs, but Bentivoglio was not prepared to put in a good word for Vivaldi with the cardinal. Furthermore,

they were unable to reach agreement on the financing of the opera season, so that finally no opera was performed in 1736. The links with Ferrara and Bentivoglio were not broken, however, and in January 1739, two of Vivaldi's operas were staged – *Siroe* and *Farnace*. Although Cardinal Ruffo was not in the city at the time, Vivaldi was not present to assist, and it so happened that a very bad harpsichord player accompanied the recitatives. Vivaldi was blamed for this and wrote a final letter to Bentivoglio to try to put matters right: "Excellency, I am at my wits' end and I cannot bear it that such a nincompoop simply fools around and so destroys my good name. I humbly beseech you not to abandon me, while I assure you that if my name is not cleared I am prepared to do anything to save my honor, for who takes away my honor takes away my life." At this, in a frigid letter, the Marquis severed for good all links with the composer.

The interior of the basilica of San Marco in Venice, painted by Canaletto (Windsor, Royal Collection). Here – before, during or after the service – music designated as "da chiesa" (church music) was played. This was distinguished from chamber music ("musica da camera").

Naples in the time of Vivaldi and Corelli in a painting by François de Nomé (Naples, private collection).

Vivaldi's last two years had dawned. He had lost his mother in 1728 and his father had died in 1736. He would only survive him by five years.

One of Vivaldi's best–known contemporaries, Arcangelo Corelli, had died in 1713. As Vivaldi later did, this composer made "tournées" through Italy and Europe with his "modern" instrumental music. His oeuvre is not large: twenty–four sonatas "da camera," twenty–four sonatas "da chiesa," twelve violin sonatas, and twelve concerti grossi. Nonetheless his work had a decisive importance for the development of baroque music and for the work of Vivaldi.

Vivaldi's famous contemporary Arcangelo Corelli in a portrait by C. Silvestri. Beside it is the first page of the manuscript of the 12 Sonate a tre, opus 1 (Venice, Biblioteca Nazionale Marciana). These sonatas (and much of Corelli's work) were first performed by the composer before they went to the printer. In this case they were sent to Rome, to the publisher Mutti, in 1681.

The basilica of San Petronio in Bologna in a 17th–century print.

Other well–known contemporaries of Vivaldi were Guiseppe Torelli (1659–1709) and his pupil Francesco Manfredini (1680–1748). They both worked in the orchestra of San Petronio in Bologna. Torelli wrote the first important *concerti grossi*. In some of these concertos the solo violin part was so important and so virtuosic that they have come to be regarded as the forerunners of the violin concerto.

Manfredini's most important work is his *opus 3: Concerti a due violini e basso continuo obbligato, e due altri violini, viola e basso di rinforzo ad abitrio, con una Pastorale per il SS. Natale.* As far as the new baroque style was concerned, in particular the violin part, these concertos have a good deal in common with Vivaldi's *L'Estro armonico*, written in 1712.

The violinist and composer, Pietro Locatelli (1695–1764), was also an important contemporary of Vivaldi's and also his friend. Locatelli was a pupil of Corelli. He worked in Berlin and Kassel before settling in Amsterdam, where he became an important figure in musical life and where his compositions were published. Besides his *concerti grossi*, his 24 *Capricci for solo violin* are well known, largely because of the important role played by the virtuosity of the violin part.

Even though in 1739 the French traveler Charles de Brosses called Vivaldi an "old man" (he was 61), until April 1740 he was as active as ever in Venice. State visits by foreign nobles to Venice were graced with his concertos and operas in the ospedali and in the theaters.

An opera performance in a Venetian theater in the time of Vivaldi.

The archives of the Ospedale della Pietà show that during these years Vivaldi sold all his new compositions to the ospedale. He was clearly planning to leave Venice and, with Anna Giraud, go to live in Vienna. He made the definite move in April 1740. In the same month he resigned his post with the Ospedale della Pietà.

Why Vienna? One reason was an invitation from Emperor Charles VI, with whom he was friendly. Moreover, he thought he could depend on the emperor's successors, Maria Theresa and her husband Franz Stephan, Duke of Lotharingan and Grand Duke of Tuscany. And finally, Vienna had become the capital of Italian opera, evidenced by the fact that the Italian librettist, Pietro Metastasio, had been appointed as the Viennese court poet in 1730.

Above: The Old Town Hall of
Amsterdam *by Pieter Saenredam
(Rijksmuseum, Amsterdam). This
building stood on the Dam from
1452 until 1652, when it burned
down. In this print the spire of the
tower has already fallen into ruin
and disappeared, which happened
in 1615. On his visit to
Amsterdam, Vivaldi was able to
see Jacob van Campen's "new"
monumental Town Hall, which
came into use in 1655 (this is now
the Royal Palace on the Dam).*

Opposite page: The street *by
Johannes Vermeer (Amsterdam,
Rijksmuseum).*

Two years before he left for Vienna, Vivaldi
was in Amsterdam on the occasion of the 100th
anniversary of the Schouwburg. On January 7,
1738, he conducted a festive opening concert
and he himself played the solo violin part of his
Concerto Grosso in D major, RV 562a. It was
probably the first time the composer visited
Amsterdam, although since 1711 his works had
been printed by the music publishers Roger and
Le Cène. It is presumed that the latter had a
hand in Vivaldi's invitation. In Amsterdam,
people presumably were not aware that Vivaldi's
prestige had suffered a considerable blow
because of the events surrounding the opera in
Ferrara and that his fame in Venice was
declining.

The then Amsterdam Schouwburg was at
Keizersgracht 384, between Runstraat and
Berenstraat. It had been opened on January 3,
1638, with a performance of Vondel's famous
play *Gijsbreght van Aemstel*. The festive program for the 100th anniversary mentioned,
among other things, the tragedy *Caesar en Cato*
and the occasional work *Het Eeuwgetyde van
den Amsteldamschen Schouwburg* (The
Centenary of the Amsterdam City Theater), both
graced by the music of various composers. A few
decades later the theater burned to the ground
during a performance on May 11, 1772. The
entrance remained, fronting the new building
which was erected a year later.

In Vienna, in 1740, Vivaldi hoped to be able
to set to work because of his good connections
with the court. Perhaps his leaving Venice was
prompted by the fear that he would not earn
enough, seeing that in the City of the Doges, like
everywhere else in Europe, there was an econo-
mic crisis. It is significant that no successor to
Vivaldi was appointed.

Unfortunately, Vivaldi's admirer, Charles VI,
died unexpectedly in October 1740. His daughter, Maria Theresa, was much less accommoda-
ting than the composer had expected. For example, after the death of the court Kapellmeister
Fux, in February 1741, he was not appointed in
his place; that honor went to the
vice–Kapellmeister.

Little is known of this last year of Vivaldi's
life. It was only discovered in 1938 that he died

Freyung Platz in Vienna, a painting by Bernardo Bellotto (Vienna, Kunsthistorisches Museum).

in Vienna and not in the city of his birth. The following facts have been established. Vivaldi found accommodation in Vienna in the house of the widow of a saddlemaker, Maria Agatha Waller (or Wahler), in the Kärntnertor, which no longer exists. He was in Vienna in February 1741, in any case, because Count Anton Ulrich von Sachsen–Meiningen twice records meetings with the "red priest" in his diary. On June 26, 1741, Vivaldi signed a receipt for Count Vinciguerra di Collalto. This concerned the receiving of 12 Hungarian gulders for "lots of music." It is the composer's last known signature. Was the money intended to enable him to leave Vienna again? Finally, there is the registra-

tion of Vivaldi's death in the register of the Stephan's Dom: *Burial Vivaldi, July 28, 1741. The Reverend Antonio Vivaldi, secular priest, died of internal fire in the Sattlerhuis in the Kärntnertor, 63 years old, [and buried] at the burial ground of the hospital.*

The "internal fire" from which Vivaldi died and from which he suffered all his life was probably asthmatic bronchitis (certainly not syphilis as was once suggested). As Mozart's would be fifty years later, his funeral was very simple, with no fuss. The costs of the funeral are recorded in the register of deaths: 2.36 for the ringing of the bell, 2.15 for the cloth on the bier, 4.30 for six bearers with cloaks, 2.00 for six lamps and a few other items. The total came to 19 florins and 45 kreutzers. As a comparison, the funeral of a nobleman cost at least 100 florins.

Above: *Vienna in a painting by Bernardo Bellotto (Vienna, Kunsthistorisches Museum).*

Below: *A receipt written out by Vivaldi for Count Vinciguerra di Collalto.*

Six choristers from the choir of the Stephan's Dom sang at the burial. Whether Joseph Haydn, then 9 years old, was present is not clear.

The following can be read in the memoirs of Pietro Gradenigo: "The priest D. Antonio Vivaldi, the phenomenal violinist, also known as the red priest, honored for his concertos and other compositions, once earned more than 50,000 ducats, he died poor in Vienna, due to his extraordinary extravagance." This is a great exaggeration. At the height of his fame Vivaldi undoubtedly earned a great deal of money, but the amount mentioned is much too high. Furthermore, he also took risks as an impresario. His household with two women probably cost him quite a bit, and his health problems also created expenses. Extravagance would appear to be an implausible explanation for the poor financial circumstances in which he found himself at the end.

Vivaldi's friend and household companion of many years' standing, the singer Anna Giraud, returned to Venice, where she died in 1750.

Vivaldi's grave in the "Spitaler Gottsacker" no longer exists because the Technical University was erected on that site. Only a memorial tablet remembers Vivaldi's short stay in Vienna.

Vienna in a painting by Franz Scheyerer (Vienna, Museen der Stadt).

The Most Important Works of Antonio Vivaldi

In the present state of Vivaldi research, there are some 750 compositions known and numbered according to the Ryoms Verzeichnis *(RV). The following overview is intended to offer a representative choice from the various categories of compositions. Compositions for which the music has not (yet) been found have not been included.*

Vocal Works

Il Mopso, for 5 voices, RV 691

La Sena Festeggiante, serenata for 3 voices, RV 693

Bajazet (Tamerlano), opera, RV 703

Catone in Utica, opera, RV 705

Dorilla in Tempo, opera, RV 709

La fida Ninfa, opera, RV 714

Giustino, opera, RV 717

Griselda, opera, RV 718

L'Incoronazione di Dario, opera, RV 719

L'Olimpiade, opera, RV 725

Orlando finto pazzo, opera, RV 727

Orlando furioso, opera, RV 728

Ottone in villa, opera, RV 729

Teuzzone, opera, RV 736

Tito Manlio, opera, RV 738

La verità in cimento, opera, RV 739

Gloria, in D major, part of a Mass, RV 589

Dixit Dominus, in D major, psalm, RV 594

Beatus vir, in G major, psalm, RV 597

Magnificat, in G minor, RV 610

Juditha Triumphans, oratorio, RV 644

Vienna in the time of Vivaldi.

(The title and opus number of the first group of works is given; the separate parts all have their own RV number which is not given.)

Instrumental Works

Sonate da camera a tre, due violini e violone o cembalo, opus 1, 12 sonatas

Sonate a violino e basso per il cembalo, opus 2, 12 sonatas

L'Estro armonico, concerti, opus 3, Libro primo: 6 concertos, Libro secondo: 6 concertos

La Stravaganza, concerti, opus 4, Libro primo: 6 concertos, Libro secondo: 6 concertos

Concerti a cinque stromenti, opus 7, Libro primo: 6 concertos, Libro secondo: 6 concertos

Il Cimento dell'Armonia e dell'Invenzione, opus 8, 12 violin concertos, nos. 9 and 12 also for oboe, nos. 1 to 4 are "The Four Seasons"

La Cetra, opus 9, 12 violin concertos, no. 9 for 2 violins

VI Concerti a flauto traverso, opus 10, 6 flute concertos

Il Pastor fido, opus 13, 6 sonatas for musette (a sort of bagpipe), vielle (hurdy-gurdy), flute, oboe or violin and continuo, probably an arrangement by another composer

Concertos for viola d'amore and orchestra, RV 392–397

Concertos for cello and orchestra, RV 398–424

Concerto for mandolin and orchestra, RV 425

Concertos for recorder and orchestra RV 441–442

Concertos for oboe and orchestra, RV 446–465

Concertos for bassoon and orchestra, RV 466–504

Double concertos, RV 531–548

for two cellos and orchestra

for two mandolins and orchestra

for two flutes and orchestra

for two oboes and orchestra

for two trumpets and orchestra

for two horns and orchestra

Concertos for three or more solo instruments and orchestra, RV 549–580

Chamber Music

Violin sonatas, RV 1–37 (opus 2 and opus 5)

Cello sonatas, RV 41–47

Flute sonatas, RV 48–51

Oboe sonata, RV 53

Trio sonatas for 2 violins and continuo, RV 60–79 (opus 1)

Sonatas for 2 instruments and continuo, RV 80–86

Concertos for various combinations of instruments,

without orchestra, RV 87–108